CW00525670

TOP TEN MYTHS ABOUT ENLIGHTENMENT

And How To Avoid Getting Trapped By Them!

HELEN HAMILTON

BALBOA.PRESS

A DIVISION OF HAY HOUSE

Balboa Press books may be ordered through booksellers or by contacting:

Balboa Press
A Division of Hay House
1663 Liberty Drive
Bloomington, IN 47403
www.balboapress.co.uk
UK TFN: 0800 0148647 (Toll Free inside the UK)
UK Local: 02036 956325 (+44 20 3695 6325 from outside the UK)

Because of the dynamic nature of the Internet, any web addresses or
links contained in this book may have changed since publication and may
no longer be valid. The views expressed in this work are solely those
of the author and do not necessarily reflect the views of the publisher,
and the publisher hereby disclaims any responsibility for them.

The author of this book does not dispense medical advice or
prescribe the use of any technique as a form of treatment for physical,
emotional, or medical problems without the advice of a physician,
either directly or indirectly. The intent of the author is only to offer
information of a general nature to help you in your quest for emotional
and spiritual well-being. In the event you use any of the information
in this book for yourself, which is your constitutional right, the author
and the publisher assume no responsibility for your actions.

Any people depicted in stock imagery provided by Getty Images are
models, and such images are being used for illustrative purposes only.
Certain stock imagery © Getty Images.

Print information available on the last page.

ISBN: 978-1-9822-8373-5 (sc)
ISBN: 978-1-9822-8374-2 (e)

Balboa Press rev. date: 06/23/2021

TABLE OF CONTENTS

Dedication

This book was written to show that everyone can reach enlightenment and that it is simply our natural state. May this book help you see that full Self-realisation is not only possible for you, but that it's your birthright.

You already have all that you need inside.

INTRODUCTION

Throughout human history, very few beings have fully awakened to the true realisation of what they are. Enlightenment has been viewed as almost impossible to achieve in our lifetime because we feel it's some distant goal that only those who have the right karma can attain. Some part of ourselves looks at the famous enlightened beings of the past and compares who we are now to that standard and of course we feel less than able to match up to their almost superhuman qualities and personalities. To become a Buddha though, we must not try to match who he was after his enlightenment but should try to match what the Buddha did to wake up fully.

We only see the end result of someone's awakening process when they are teaching, holding Satsang or have become well known. We often forget they had to go through a process too and it's the process itself we should want to know more about...not the end result. Only viewing the enlightened beings as we see them after their awakening can be confusing to us because we may try to emulate what they are now. To get what they have and to live as they live, we must do what they *did* and *NOT* what they *do* now.

The aim of this book is to reveal some errors in thinking about enlightened beings that are causing many to fail along the pathway to enlightenment. These errors in our thinking may also cause us to not even begin the journey because we don't feel worthy or able to achieve what the great teachers have done. It stands to reason that Krishna, Christ, the Buddha and all other genuine awakened beings started their journey as average human beings just like us. To fully awaken to the reality of what they are, they had to overcome some myths about enlightenment. This book will summarise these vital things to know.

Each myth is explained and exposed and you will come to see how and why it is not true. As you read each chapter, your belief and courage will strengthen and you should come to see that these great beings that we emulate began exactly where we are today. You will also come to see that what they achieved is available to you…right here, right now.

CHAPTER I

Myth 1: Enlightened Beings are Selfless, Altruistic and self-sacrificing

FACT: Enlightened beings are selfish and self-centred just like everyone else! They are completely self-absorbed and interested in themselves.

Enlightened beings such as Christ, Mother Teresa, the Buddha and more have long since been admired for their seeming ability to selflessly serve others, and their complete and total compassion. We've come to regard them as having superhuman abilities the average person does not have. We feel they have somehow learned to put their own needs aside and focus only on others, but this is not true. Indeed, some pathways believe this so completely that they teach selfless service as a means to reaching enlightenment.

All human beings begin by being self-centred, egotistical and concerned only with their own wants and needs. This is a basic fact of human existence and it has been this way in order to allow us to grow into adolescence and eventually adulthood. If you doubt this fact at all, simply observe a two year old toddler having a tantrum, or a teenager being asked to help with household chores. Part of learning to function as an adult involves learning to put the needs of others before our own sometimes, and being able to delay the gratification of our desires. Somehow, a myth has arisen that enlightened beings have completely mastered that skill and they never think about what they want and what is best for them.

Consider how selfless it was of Christ to take himself off alone to the desert for forty days to test himself against temptation. It was actually quite a selfish thing to do! To ignore what others wanted of him and be willing to spend as long as it took alone in the desert to prove his enlightenment to himself was quite self-centred. Consider how much opposition you would get from friends, family, co-workers and your boss if you went to work on Monday and announced you were taking forty 40 days off starting now to go contemplate and meditate alone!

Buddha, too, was only thinking of himself when he sat down under the Bodhi tree and decided to sit for as long as it took to be completely enlightened. There are many stories and records of beings taking themselves off to quiet or isolated places to meditate and finally transcend the mind. All these beings had an ability to be completely and totally selfish when needed. This is something we shy away from in modern day society because we feel it's irresponsible and impractical to do. Where would we be if the Buddha had said, "I really don't have time today to sit down under this tree. There are other jobs I need to do first. It's selfish of me to want to be alone and reach enlightenment." How different would our world be today if this had been what he said?

So, why do we feel enlightened beings are selfless and self-sacrificing? Where did this idea come from? The idea that all awakened beings are selfless and work tirelessly to serve all mankind is really not true. These great beings serve themselves only...the difference is they were VERY sure about what their own "*self*" was. They investigated what their "self" was until it was clear, simple and obvious to them that when they said "myself", they meant all of existence and its source. Their concept of "Self" had to grow to include all life, in all its sentient *and* insentient forms, because they knew it was themselves.

What appears to be selfless behaviour in an awakened being is really only the outcome of knowing that all that you see, feel and experience is you. Knowing so clearly and deeply that there is only you, wherever you go and whatever you do, appears as deep concern for the wellbeing of all. The awakened being knows however that there are no others at all! They have been so self-centred that they have totally eradicated the concept of "other" or "else" or "different to me". They did this by completely self-enquiring until it was stunningly clear just what they actually were.

The concepts of selfish and selfless seem to be opposites to most human beings, but to an awakened being they are actually totally irrelevant. There is no "me" separate to all other beings and all existence. There is nothing "other" than you, and there never was. Enlightened beings live from a place of total oneness, knowing there is only the Self, but to people who are not yet totally awake to this, it appears they are completely selfless. Doesn't it make sense that if you knew every human being was you, that you would also begin to feel love and concern for them and their experience? Doesn't it make sense that you would begin to see all life as an aspect of your own self and value it just as much as yours? You would begin to see that anything you do to "others" you are really doing to yourself.

Of course I am not suggesting we ignore or neglect others, or in any way cause them harm. But we DO need to learn to focus more consistently on what we want. We need to do what the Buddha did (metaphorically of course…as not many people can sit still in the lotus position for that long!). We have been doing what we THOUGHT the Buddha did, but not what he actually put his time towards. Once our work is done for the day, it is totally ok to spend as much time as you can and want on your own pathway. We can know that every effort we put forward towards our own enlightenment will benefit not only ourselves but all those around us too. If you doubt this then look at the effect the Buddha had on others once he was awake. How many other beings did Christ affect with his wisdom, love and compassion? Too many to count and still going!

Being selfish and self-centred is not always a bad thing, yet it has come to always be viewed as such in our society. Let's stop trying to reach some idealised picture of what we *think* it takes to reach enlightenment and start doing what those great beings actually did. Only that way will we finally get the same results as they did. It's time to put to bed the idea that reaching towards enlightenment is wrong, irresponsible and not helping others. It is, in fact, our birthright to wake up fully and see what we really are. Never before has it been easier to enlighten, as more teachers awaken and we have resources to travel to see those teachers. We have the internet too in this day and age so we can read books such as this without ever meeting the teacher face to face if it is not yet possible. Consider how "selfish" awakened beings had to be in the past by spending one, two or twelve years (or a whole lifetime) with a teacher and having to leave their work, family and old life behind to sit with that teacher. Now we simply click a button on a computer screen and an enlightened teacher comes to us or their words come through our letter box or onto our screen. We can even listen to a teacher's words whilst doing our daily work or driving our kids to school. There really is no excuse not to be the best version of you!

CHAPTER 2

Myth 2: Enlightened Beings Have Totally Overcome All Desires for Sensory Pleasures and Do Not Try to Feel Good

Fact: Enlightened beings love to feel pleasure and are very hedonistic. They are so addicted to feeling good that they sought out the only permanent way to feel good all the time!

The basic drive for all of our human behaviour is the urge to feel good, or to feel better than we do right now. If we closely examine all our habits and distractions, what we do for entertainment, where we go on vacation and what we desire, we will find that all of this is done for one reason only — *to feel good*. Whether we are watching tv or shopping for clothes, we are doing it to distract ourselves from our worries and to feel better than we do. All our basic human drives are aimed at helping us to feel loved, safe and happy. Take a moment to think of all the ways we try to feel good as human beings; some are safer and easier than others but all of the following are indulged in because we think they will make us feel better. Humans always seek out pleasure in all its forms and are programmed to avoid pain at all costs. Here are some of the ways we do this:

- Drinking alcohol
- Taking part in sports
- Shopping (of any kind)
- Eating
- Having sex
- Socialising
- Taking drugs
- Listening to music
- Watching tv, movies or playing video games
- Dancing
- Art, ballet, theatre and similar
- Having a family
- Getting married
- Being in a relationship
- Seeking enlightenment

We could go on and on here. All of our lives, we are driven by this desire for pleasure and to avoid the pain of loneliness and feeling negative emotions. If you examine your life, you may be surprised. We may even try to reach enlightenment because we've heard tales of feeling peace, bliss and joy and that sounds a whole lot better than our everyday, average boredom and frustration with how life is right now.

If we can own this tendency within ourselves to seek pleasure, then we can begin to work with it. Most spiritual seekers are trying to reject this urge when in reality, it is the most direct path to enlightenment. We have somehow believed the idea that to be enlightened is to totally have overcome this urge for pleasure. We may have read scriptures telling us to ignore our senses and the pleasure we can get from them, and focus only on the Truth of our being. We have become convinced that the Buddha and other enlightened beings had a superhuman ability to focus only on the Truth and turn away from pleasure.

The Sage of enlightenment has more in common with the hedonist than the ascetic that renounces everything in the world! The hedonist seeks pleasure and devotes their life to it whilst the ascetic renounces anything that can give pleasure and instead choses a disciplined and solitary life with no possessions. The lifestyle of the ascetic has come to be regarded as necessary for reaching enlightenment but it is, in fact, directly going against human behaviour.

If you stop and think about it for a moment, it will begin to become clear that even myths one and two alone have probably stopped millions of people from reaching for enlightenment because they felt they had to overcome two of the most basic human tendencies to do so! The popular myths are that each awakened being somehow gained superhuman powers to be able to do things that the average person cannot. Few of us can live like monks or nuns and give up the pub on a Saturday night; but we do not need to! If we can simply learn how the enlightened beings used these human desires for pleasure we need not avoid anything or strive to overcome; but rather to direct those urges into a much more productive way.

I am not suggesting here that we begin to indulge every whim and fancy we have ever had but rather to do what the Sages do and find the highest, easiest and most reliable source of pleasure. The Sages know that to seek pleasure from external sources will only leave us wanting more, so they chose to find the greatest pleasure within themselves. Consider for a moment how good it feels to indulge in chocolate, to listen to music and sing at the top of your voice, to try on a new suit or sit in front of your new giant flat screen tv. All these feel good momentarily, but after a very short time the pleasure is gone; the chocolate is gone, the music is over and the tv does not have that "new" feeling anymore. Now we must repeat the same thing to try and get another moment's pleasure.

The enlightened beings realised something very important and they applied it to their lives. I want to share it with you now. They realised the pleasure we get from indulging in these things does not come from the thing itself, but rather from the absence of thoughts and desires while you are indulging in it. Consider that when you are eating chocolate, you are not desiring chocolate, so you feel good. When you are singing and dancing you are feeling good because you are ignoring all other thoughts in your mind. The Sages knew this so they looked for the most direct and permanent means to gain pleasure and to continuously experience it. So is it possible to feel peaceful and happy all the time? Yes it is if we do not depend upon any external thing to make us happy, because when it's gone we will again be unhappy. Our own happiness is available to us anytime we want to access it if we simply look at what is really here and what we really are.

The awakened ones have realised that when we focus on the truth of our being, we will feel good and the more we focus on that truth the better we will feel. The truth is that there is only you and there is nothing other than you. All that you see, feel and experience is you. When we believe ourselves to be separate and different from everything and everyone else we believe that there are lots of other things "out there". Some of these things we want because we imagine they will make us feel happier, safer and more loved. Some of these things we do not want because we imagine they will make us feel worse. But the truth is that there is nothing outside ourself; all is within us but we imagine a boundary or barrier between "me" and "everything else". When the truth is seen that there is only you, then you will also see that none of your thoughts are true either. If there has only ever been you, then nothing can hurt you, nor can you die or become ill. You are all of creation and you are the creator. And in fact, those two are the same One expressing itself.

When you can no longer believe any of your thoughts you will feel at peace all the time and nothing can bring you out of that state. True enlightenment is the best way to feel good all the time because it is simply your natural state. Of course, awakened beings loved truth because it is true but they also realised that they are trying to achieve the exact same thing as the drug addict or the compulsive spender; we are all trying to feel as high as we can and as good as we can. The only difference is in the method. Enlightenment brings total clarity and peace and there are no come downs or side effects. If human beings are destined to seek pleasure and to avoid pain, isn't it sensible to seek the best, highest and the only permanent source of pleasure? Wouldn't it make sense to choose a source of pleasure that can never run out, hurt you or be taken away by anything or anyone?

Wouldn't it make sense to choose a lasting source of pleasure that is also beneficial to everyone you meet and come into contact with? The Saints, Sages and Enlightened beings of this world uplift the rest of the world with their love, energy and relentless insistence that we are all the One being experiencing itself through countless human beings and other forms.

CHAPTER 3

Myth 3: Enlightened Beings Know a Lot of Things That Everyone Else Doesn't

Fact: Enlightened beings know only ONE thing! They have remembered only one thing over and over again. They have forgotten everything else and they do not value knowledge or learning in the way we think.

There is a huge myth in the human population which says that in order to reach enlightenment we have to study a long time and learn lots of things. We have somehow come to view enlightened beings as having gained lots of secrets about how the world works, how we work, what we really are and much more. Many people believe that awakening can only truly occur if we have spent many lifetimes studying lots of different spiritual techniques and can do lots of yogic postures and meditate in many different styles. We may also believe that we need to know lots of mantras, hand postures (mudras) and countless other bits of information before we can fully wake up to the truth of our being.

The fact is that all this is simply not the case. Enlightened beings know only ONE fact...and that is *there is nothing other than the Self.* There is no other than you. All that you see is you. Every human being, plant, animal and insentient and sentient life form is you. Awakened beings have become very proficient at forgetting about everything else and everyone else. They do not know any special facts or knowledge and they do not value book learning or scholarly scriptural studies. In fact all of these things can be nothing but a huge distraction from the truth.

Once you realise through self-inquiry that you cannot find anything or anyone else except you, then you simply need to hold on to this fact and keep experiencing it. Enlightened beings are simply the ones that have discovered this fact and remembered it consistently, until they only operated from a level of wholeness and completeness. There are no tricks or techniques to learn, there are no secrets or good karma needed to awaken. There are simply those beings that are willing to stay with this one simple fact for as long as it takes. In some ways, enlightened beings are the simplest of us all, the least clever of us all, the least academically minded because they value simplicity and provable truth. To read about someone else's awakening and hundreds of paths to enlightenment is simply not necessary or helpful.

So how does this myth stop us from waking up? It intimidates us into thinking we are not capable of waking up to the truth of our being fully. If we needed to be very clever and intelligent, along with having lots of spiritual knowledge, then most of us would stand no chance of reaching enlightenment. If we needed to be able to stand on our heads for hours on end or to sit in the lotus position for a long time to reach enlightenment, a lot of us would have to give up right now. Knowing this myth is not true is very inspiring because it means that anyone can wake up fully and completely and no special skills are needed.

Even better than the fact that we only need to remember one thing consistently is that no awakened being was able to be consistent when they first started! Each being that has reached full enlightenment was just as inconsistent and unable to concentrate as we may be right now. They simply kept working at it, and when they forgot the one fact they needed to remember (the knowing that there is only One being and not many) they simply reminded themselves over and over. If these skills are the only ones needed to reach Self-Realisation, then we should all celebrate as it is a lot easier than we may have thought.

Why have a lot of beings tried and failed to reach enlightenment? Why has it become associated as being very difficult and hard to do? Because we all believed these myths, and when we believe them, we have to experience them as true! Simply reading through these myths and the facts that are actually true will boost your confidence in your own ability. You would not be reading a book like this if you were not destined to enlighten yourself!

Forget everything else you think you know about yourself, the Self, Enlightenment and remember the one thought — there is only you.

CHAPTER 4

Myth 4: You Have to Surrender Everything to Reach Enlightenment

FACT: Enlightened beings did not surrender anything! Instead, they simply investigated deeply whether there actually was anything to surrender!

There is another huge myth in the spiritual seeker's mind that says you have to surrender all your personal thoughts and beliefs about life, the Self and everything before you can awaken to the Truth of what you are and live as that Truth. This myth causes a lot of unnecessary pain because we may feel we have to give up some beliefs and thoughts that mean a lot to us. Human beings are hardwired to want to hold onto things that are familiar to them so it seems like a great effort and sacrifice to give up thoughts that we like or are familiar with. Even if we have beliefs that we don't like and that make us feel bad (such as "I am not good enough") we can still find we have some strange loyalty to them just because they are familiar.

The myth pervades human consciousness that to reach enlightenment, the Sages have had to find superhuman strength of character in order to be able to let go of these thoughts. The idea also exists that it takes time to surrender every single thought we have and that some thoughts are easier than others to let go of. But what if that is simply not true? What if the awakened ones found another way around this conundrum?

Awakening to the Self becomes progressively more effortless as you advance through higher levels of consciousness to find that which is beyond all levels. So if you find yourself with a seemingly very hard thing to do spiritually, then it may help to know that there must be another way around the issue that is much easier.

Enlightened beings have just deeply investigated whether all the thoughts we have about ourselves are actually true, useful and worth keeping. At the end of their investigations each time, it was found that no thoughts were true at all, not on the fullest level of Enlightenment. Thoughts began to slow down simply because these beings were not valuing their mind and thoughts at all. There is nothing wrong with thoughts and with our mind. It is totally helpful when it comes to navigating through daily life, our work and our family life. The mind has very little useful input, though, on what we really are because it is not able to see that which is beyond the mind. As we investigate more and more what we are by having a direct experience of it, we will naturally come to feel peace, joy, love, bliss and stillness more often. As we welcome the silent, still peace of the direct experience of Self, we will find that less and less do we value thinking about the Self. Even when thinking occurs it will be more often in the background of our awareness, rather than at the forefront.

Awakened beings never surrendered any thought at all, but rather they just became too lazy to bother focusing on any one thought. They would rather focus on the love, the peace, the open, silent awareness that they are. In that beautiful, open place of being yourself, the mind's chatter becomes silent. But not because you have forced yourself to let go of anything. It becomes progressively more silent because less and less is it of any value to you! It is easy to ignore something or to let go of something if it means nothing to you. Consider how many noises you are hearing right now, as you read this, yet are paying no attention to them! We naturally learn to not notice noises in our environment that are normal, usual and not relevant to us (such as cars passing, dogs barking, rain on the window etc). Thoughts and a noisy mind can be just like this too.

Instead of climbing an impossible mountain of letting go of all thoughts, see if they still have value to you when you rest in that silent space of awareness. Then you won't need courage, conviction or anything else that your mind says you need to wake up fully. You won't even remember what you thought you had to do at one point, you will just be so in love with the peace.

You cannot stop valuing and paying attention to thoughts just like that, but you CAN start paying attention to the silence instead. Naturally and effortlessly over time you will be distracted by your mind less and less and you won't even care that you have not surrendered a thing! Be lazy like the awakened Sages!

CHAPTER 5

Myth 5: You Have to Go Through a Death Experience or Your Ego Has to Die to Reach Enlightenment

FACT: Nothing dies at all. There is no ego death but only expansion of what we know we are. Enlightened beings sidestep this ego death to realise nothing ever dies.

One of the most damaging myths that pervades the mind of spiritual students is that at some point there is some big showdown finale between the Self and the ego and that to reach full enlightenment you have to face your worst fear and go through some death experience. This is simply not the case at all. Let's look at how and why this myth may have come about and look at how to work around it. Very few of us have the courage it would take to be willing to die (unless we were suffering so badly) to wake up fully. In my own journey and in helping others, I have not only found this myth to be untrue, but also the very idea of it scares people into avoiding awakening.

Firstly, it may help to look at what the ego actually is. In the spiritual world the ego is simply the tendency to believe we are a separate and limited being, it is the belief that "I am this body and mind". Really, the ego is just ONE THOUGHT that says "I am ONLY this body and mind".

The ego actually "dies" the very first moment we realise we may be more than that and accept that we are the unlimited Infinite Being. Once we have experienced even once the great Silence that we are, we can no longer totally go back to believing "All I am is this mind and body". Now we may seem to go back and forth at first between the belief of being a separate being and being the Self; but we can never truly forget. What does this mean in our spiritual practice then? It means that the great "ego death" you may be fearing has already happened and you may not even have noticed it!

Ego is simply the tendency to self-define and the very first moment we notice we may be more than we realised, that self-definition gets an upgrade. The ego then does not have to die but come to accept, "There is more to me than I have been believing". There is an ending of sorts but it is only that we can no longer believe that we are ONLY this mind and body. That is not a fearsome thing at all and in fact it can be quite blissful! We change our mind very often about things, it is an inherent human trait. The feared "ego death" comes down to a simple revelation of, "I have a whole bunch of thoughts in my head based on what I thought I was and now I see they are no longer relevant to me".

Consider for a moment if you were somehow convinced you were Chinese and yet all of your friends were telling you that you are French. You suddenly see you were born in France, you speak French, you are living in France and you have never been to China! How much courage would you have to muster to let the belief die that you were Chinese? None at all — because it would be simply obvious. You would say, "Oh I was so confused! All my life I thought I was Chinese but now I see that was silly because I am so obviously French!" It is the same with Self-Realisation too — the moment we realise we are more than we thought we were, it is easy to let go of the old ideas of what we were.

So how has this myth come into being? Sometimes on the pathway of surrender (rather than knowledge, etc) we may start to believe that we have to give up one thing before we can experience another; we may believe we have to give up our old self-definition before we can experience what we really are. It is much easier to simply let our mind think whatever it wants to and in the meantime directly experience what we really are through self-inquiry and contemplation. (See my other books and free teachings on my website for examples.) Once we directly experience what we actually are, it takes no courage at all to let go of what we used to think we were.

Remember, the ego is just one thought! It is the thought that "I am only this mind and body". Awakened beings have avoided any confrontation and showdown and simply realised that "I am the formless awareness that was never

23

born and can never die. Death is not an actual possibility for me." You cannot hold onto both these thoughts; you cannot believe you are only one body and mind when you keep experiencing the greater truth. Enlightened Sages have simply swapped one self-definition for the other and no courage was involved at all. It's time to put this myth to rest finally and to know the truth. All that occurs along a spiritual pathway to Enlightenment is your definition of what you know yourself to be is based on actual experience and not belief. Nobody can ever experience that they are actually only one mind and body, but they can imagine convincingly they are. You CAN prove what you really are by direct experience through self-inquiry. Once you have proved it to yourself, it is easy to let go of old ideas. Out with the old and in with the new.

CHAPTER 6

Myth 6: You Have to Be Very Patient to Reach Enlightenment Because It Takes a Very Long Time. Enlightened Beings Have a Lot of Patience

FACT: Enlightened Beings are only interested in what is happening now. They have no patience at all for a time in the future and they have no interest in getting anywhere or reaching any goals.

Myth number six has come into our consciousness because we have focused more on what enlightenment looks like AFTER we reach it and we are trying to emulate those who have already achieved it. There is a false idea in human consciousness that all awakened beings are totally ok with everything and have infinite patience but if we look closer we will begin to realise that enlightened beings are not as patient as we may think. Perhaps they are the most impatient beings of us all because they are unable and unwilling to accept any level of falsehood or illusion. Awakened beings are very impatient to get to the truth of what they are.

Along with awakening comes an awareness that time and space do not exist in the way we think they do. Awakening will show us that our past, present and future are really figments of our imagination and a function of memory. All there is in reality is this moment, right now, and those that have reached enlightenment have learned to always respect that. There is no point in avoiding looking at something that needs our attention because the only time we will have to do it is now. Even if we call it "tomorrow" it will still be "now" when we actually get to tomorrow. Nobody has ever really experienced yesterday or tomorrow because when they do it looks and feels like now.

So it can be said that enlightened beings have very little patience or faith because they do not put stock in the idea of a future. The idea of time and progress has infected our pathway so much that we may really feel that unless we have been meditating or seeking enlightenment for at least twenty years we are not anywhere near close. Perhaps it used to take a long time for people to awaken to the truth, but it need not now. In this day and age we can connect with a teacher on the other side of the world and advance our understanding; whereas at one time we may have had to leave our homes and families to travel and live with a teacher. Now we have the internet, email, video conferencing, air travel and so much more.

We also must be careful to think it takes many lifetimes to wake up to the truth. The only moment we have to realise the truth is now. Although the myth of reincarnation is hugely popular in spiritual culture, it is NOT the ultimate truth. If we are not careful we can be lulled into believing we are six, ten or one hundred lifetimes away from awakening to the truth and reaching enlightenment. If that were true then you would not be reading this book! Only someone destined to reach enlightenment would be reading a book such as this.

Set aside ideas of progress and future achievements then focus on what you can experience and prove right now. If Truth is true it must be real and provable to you right now. Awakened beings have simply kept their focus consistently on the moment that we are experiencing now. In fact, there is not a series of now moments that are joined together to create a sense of time passing; but instead there is only the One continuous now; the now goes on forever in one unbroken moment. What does that mean for you? It means that what is here right now must have been here forever and will never go. It means that when we actually look and cannot find a separate being called "me" that is alone and moving through time and space, it must never have existed. It also means that when we DO find our formless and timeless Self in this moment it must have always been here.

When you realise that anything you cannot find in this moment must not be real then you have no need of patience or faith. Both patience and faith are of the future; a promise of something bearing fruit some time ahead of now. The

Sages of old had realised that all we can ever do is explore what is actually present right now and come to understand what that actually is. When you see a picture or statue of a Buddha seated in meditation, that is exactly what they are doing; they are enjoying this moment in its fullness and completeness. They have totally given up trying to get somewhere and reach a "higher stage" or state. They have seen that enlightenment must be a total ability to focus only on what is here right now. What is here right now is here always and can never disappear because "now" cannot disappear. You are what is here right now.

Even people who have a short attention span can reach enlightenment when they see it is only a consistent focus on the reality of now, rather than a constant trying to get away from now (as most people are doing). There is no need to be patient and wait for some future moment that will never come. Realise it now and be free. Release this idea from your consciousness that you are not patient enough as yet and stop beating yourself up because you are not able to focus on anything for a great length of time. None of us can do that! Least of all awakened beings! They are totally fixated in this moment and have released all memory and anticipation of the future. Those thoughts may still occur in their brain for a while but they pay them no attention. Awakened beings are too impatient to wait for enlightenment because they want it now and can see no reason at all why they should not enjoy the fruits of this moment.

Ask yourself what is really here, right now in this moment, and just listen. Do not listen to anything in particular but just listen and see what you find. Don't wait any longer for some future enlightenment. There is a reason you do not like waiting! There is a reason you perhaps do not seem to be making much progress in your awakening. All these ideas have kept you from the Truth. If you want what the Buddha had, then you must do as he did and that was to focus on what was true right now.

CHAPTER 7

Myth 7: Enlightened Beings Have Let Go of All Attachments With a Superhuman Will Power

FACT: There is no such thing as attachments and you cannot be attached to anything; nor can you detach yourself from it!

The subject of "attachments" is another great spiritual myth that is very deeply believed by most spiritual seekers along the pathway, and it causes us so much misery if we believe this. The myth is that we start on our spiritual journey with attachments to lots of people, things and places. Somehow it has come to be believed that to reach enlightenment we must undo and detach ourselves from these burdens and be free. When we believe this myth we waste so much time and energy trying to undo something that never existed in the way we think. Awakened beings have not found some superhuman ability to let go of all worldly attachments to reach enlightenment. They simply came to see that they have always been the Self. The Self is all that there is and includes all the things we may have thought we were attached to. It is impossible to give up an attachment to something or someone when we have never been separate to it!

Let's use an example of a romantic relationship to make it clearer. In a lot of spiritual pathways, relationships are frowned upon (among other things) as it is believed it can lead to an attachment to that person which will distract us from our pathway. An attachment is a kind of energetic bond which is strengthened the more we think about that person. The idea that we have to give up an attachment to this special person in our lives may be too much for a lot of people and they begin to feel they can never do what it takes to reach enlightenment.

Awakened beings came to see that they are the formless awareness which is everywhere all the time. The nature of formlessness is that it has no substance, it is not solid or tangible, and therefore cannot get attached to anything. Only a form is able to be attached to another form — and in truth everything is the formless awareness. The great awakened beings of the past and present have come to see that attachment (and therefore detachment) is not actually possible! They simply saw this and then stopped wasting time being attached to or detached from things and people. Whatever we thought we were attached to, we can now see we are not and have never been. Whether we have been dependent on someone or something in our minds, we can come to see that this cannot be true for the Self. There simply is nothing other than the Self to be attached to! There is only the Self.

It may also help to look at the subject of "detachment" too. Detachment is the idea that when we are sufficiently spiritually advanced, we can "go back into the world" and interact with all the things, people and places that used to cause us to become attached. The idea now is that we are detached from these and we can use them or spend time with them without any ability to need them to make us happy. But this is still also perpetuating a myth because you cannot be detached from something that does not exist outside of or separate to you. To be detached from something, that must mean there are two things; there must be you and what you are detached from. My experience and that of every other awakened being contradicts this; there is only you. There is only the Self.

Once this myth has been exposed for you, then you will be able to stop wasting time, energy and resources to free yourself from an impossible situation. The more you believe you have attachments that you need to transcend before you can reach enlightenment, the more you will experience that as true. You will try harder to let go of things that you never even picked up in the first place, spiritually speaking. You may even exhaust yourself trying to do the impossible. Once you come to know that all that exists is you and that nothing is separate to you, then you will put to rest this myth of attachment and detachment once and for all. There isn't anything else to be attached to or detached from.

33

There are no huge hurdles to overcome before we can wake up to the truth of our nature. There is no mountain to climb first. We simply need to see what we really are and then to live as that in a very simple way.

CHAPTER 8

Myth 8: Awakened Beings Have Learned to Sit In the Lotus Position and Meditate All Day to Reach Enlightenment

FACT: Being good at meditation and enlightenment are not the same thing. You can become a very good meditator and not be enlightened! Awakened beings have actually become the meditation, or you could say that their life is a constant meditation.

When we start our journey to awakening, we may begin by sitting down to meditate at certain points of the day and there is nothing wrong with that. Most of us need to set aside some time to just be with ourselves in meditation initially, and this is how most of us first experience that there is something about us that is already beyond the body and mind. This is a healthy practise to do, but we must not limit our meditation to only certain times during the day. The awakened beings of the past and present have not simply become very good at meditating for long periods of the day.

Rather than meditating at a certain time or in a particular way, meditation can and must develop into a constant practice. This does not mean we try to walk around with our eyes closed, but that we come to love and prefer the actual experience of what is really happening rather than spending all our time thinking about what is happening. Awakened beings have come to be in an open energetic stance of curiosity about what life, our self and the world actually is. Most human beings live only experiencing what they think about themselves, the world and life. We believe what we think and our body has to experience the result of that thought as an emotional response.

Enlightened beings are in a constant contemplation of reality. They are unable to come to a conclusion about what reality is or what they are. They have come to consistently and totally prefer to actually experience life rather than only thinking about it. They did not make thoughts wrong or try to get rid of them, but came to see that thinking about life is only one way to experience it and will keep us suffering and feeling bad if it is our only option. Contemplation is a kind of open and active meditation that is done by questioning what we are, what the world is and what life is. We can question if what we think about life is actually true. When we ask a question of life, we can begin to notice answers that come as a thought, a revelation or epiphany and differing emotional states as a result. If we continue to gently hold the question we will begin to experience a deeper experiential answer to the question. We will begin to experience what we actually are; the formless awareness that is everywhere and everything.

Eventually all beings will come to prefer the direct and actual experience of life rather than only thinking about it. When we can realise that we have previously only been experiencing what we think about what is happening we are able to break free. Then we have a choice to actually experience life OR to think about it. Enlightenment is when we do not prefer either one or make either way of seeing the world wrong. There are times to think about things and times to actually experience life.

Enlightened beings like the Buddha may be depicted in statues seated in the lotus posture but such statues are really representing the awakened beings' state of constant inner contemplation or meditation. This inner questioning and experiencing the answer directly has come to be their life. Their life is the constant unfolding of the answer to their question. Contemplation or meditation in this way has become effortless and habitual to them, and they are exerting no effort anymore to achieve it; although they had to exert effort to keep bringing attention back at first to the direct experience of the answer.

If we take a commonly asked question such as "What am I?", we can receive different kinds of answers. We will receive thought, emotional and experiential answers too.

If we can notice our tendency is to stop at the thought answers only, or to think there is only one answer to the question, then we are already quite enlightened. Awakened beings have simply come to not accept any answer as a final answer; they have come to see that existence itself is a constant and beautiful unfolding of the answer to this wonderful question. Whether awakened beings never sit down and formally meditate ever again or they spend long periods of time alone with their eyes closed lost in bliss, we must be sure to understand they are in a state of constant questioning and never fully knowing.

CHAPTER 9

Myth 9: Enlightened Beings Are Unable to Cope With the World and Live a Normal Life. They Must Stay Withdrawn From the World and Their Previous Life

FACT: Living in the awakened way actually makes you more available for life. You will have more energy, motivation and all that is needed and you will probably end up doing exactly the same things you did before enlightenment but you will do it in peace, love and joy.

The myth that enlightenment makes you less functional (or even in some cases non-functional) has been perpetuated in our society due to the most common examples of awakened beings being teachers. You don't necessarily have to teach other beings how to wake up once you are enlightened, and in fact most people do not. Not many enlightened beings make good teachers; just as being French is not adequate to become a French teacher to

English speakers. What this does mean is that most beings who wake up to the Truth of their nature continue to live the same life as before but do not suffer anymore, ever. The vast majority of beings who are awakened simply and quietly go about their life in joy. Unfortunately for us, this means that the only examples of enlightenment are those that teach how to reach it and all we remember is a few very great beings who had large followings of people that totally dedicated their lives to teaching.

Most people have come to view enlightenment as something that effectively puts an end to our old way of living and functioning and we have come to imagine it means we cannot live at home with our families, work normal jobs and do normal human things. This myth has been intensified also because enlightenment has been seen as something that can only happen when we leave our life, pack up and live in an ashram, monastery, the mountains or a cave somewhere away from society. We have come to believe that enlightenment makes us special, different from others and necessitates special treatment. Most of us feel we are sure we would know an awakened being if we walked past one; that we would be able to tell immediately who they are, but this is simply not the case. We imagine they would be sitting on top of a mountain and have long hair and a beard or perhaps long robes and lots of people around them. The reality is that you have probably met someone who woke up to the truth of their being and you didn't know it because they weren't shouting about it. Enlightenment makes us totally normal because it takes us right back to our natural state of peace, bliss and joy. Beings living in the natural state would probably not be as recognisable as we would like to think. They would have no need or ability to shout of their achievement because they have come to see they are everywhere and they have not personally achieved anything.

The shop assistant and the pub owner are just as likely to be the next Buddha. The woman that lives across the road from you, the man you see every day at work and say hello to, the ageing old woman that lives next door to your mother-in-law or even the postman could be enlightened and most of us would never know. Enlightenment leaves us deeply functional and available for life and to life. We will find that we can be clear headed in a situation that others would panic in, we can be forgiving when we need to be or direct enough to say what we need to say. Enlightenment will allow you to actively participate in your own life rather than living in a virtual reality of thoughts inside your own mind. Most of us are missing out on the best bits of life because we are so caught up in what we think is happening. Even when sitting in a beautiful meadow or a white sand beach we will be thinking about something else and missing the moment. In the fully awakened state we will find ourselves fully present and unable to avoid or resist life. We will have more energy and time than we need and we will generally enjoy better health and our relationships will improve.

It is time for us to put away the myth that we can only pursue enlightenment if we do not like or want a normal life, because this is simply not the case. One of the greatest benefits of living in the awakened way is that we can finally just enjoy wherever we are and whatever we are doing, without the constant need to try to change everything.

Lastly for this chapter, let's look at the difference between a state of consciousness and enlightenment. Many yogis and meditators are very good at reaching some very nice states of consciousness that lead to a deep peace, bliss and stillness that makes them not want to move or participate in life. Non-functional states of consciousness in which we go into a deeper state inside ourselves is not enlightenment. Many people have confused these states with enlightenment. Some people can reach states in which they cannot feed themselves or remember their own name for a while, but this is not enlightenment. It is important to know the difference so we do not waste time on our pathway. Awakened beings are not interested in any state that will come and then go, nor do they want to live in a state that takes a lot of effort to maintain. Enlightenment is not something we do or become, but something we come to see we always were. Enlightenment recognises itself. This is in stark contrast to a state that comes and goes and affects your body and mind temporarily.

Your awakening is not complete until it has pervaded all of your life, goals, dreams, relationships, finances and work. Only when doing normal and "mundane" things brings you just as much joy as sitting in deep meditation or Satsang is your awakening complete. When you are just as happy digging the weeds in the garden, hoovering, paying your bills, driving in rush hour or meditating, then you are very much in the natural state.

CHAPTER 10

Myth 10: Enlightened Beings Transcended All Their Negative Karma Before They Reached Enlightenment

FACT: An awakened being has had to work through all of their negative karmic tendencies just like everyone else. Most enlightened beings are still working through their karmic tendencies after enlightenment for a while. They didn't get any free passes.

There is a myth that pervades human consciousness that says that if someone has reached enlightenment it is because they transcended all of their karmic baggage in a previous lifetime. This is a damaging myth to most spiritual seekers because it is simply not true and because it makes us feel as if we have no chance at fully waking up to who we really are if we still have some traits or tendencies we would like to let go of. Enlightened beings of the past and present have had just as many negative things happen to them in this lifetime as anyone else (and sometimes a lot more) but they have simply learned how to use these life events to help them transcend their mind and let go of repeating the same old ways of behaving and being. This is important to know because it means that enlightened beings are really no different to anyone else, except maybe for the fact that they made a decision inside themselves at some point to consistently use every event that made them suffer to their advantage. They decided to look at their thoughts and feelings about things that happened to them each time something negative came up. They did this every time until negative thoughts and emotions ceased and they found they could not suffer.

A lot of spiritual seekers fall into the trap of trying to clear up all their karmic patterns before they try to reach enlightenment, but this is simply not necessary. As our awakening deepens within us, it will first work through our understanding of ourselves and then it will begin to heal our mind, body, relationships, finances and every other area of our life that we allow it. Enlightenment is not really complete until we have noticed our outer world is reflecting back to us the harmonious and simple truth of what we are. This is in fact a good guidepost as to when we can let go of needing to self-inquire, contemplate or meditate any more. This is also what every awakened being has done. You are the formless awareness and you are invisible, intangible and everywhere. All that you see, feel, taste and experience in life is your reflection. The world "out there" is really your mirror image;

it is what you look like as existence itself when you see and experience yourself through human senses.

Whatever we believe about ourselves, the world and even the Self must be reflected back to us in our body, mind, emotions and world. This happens because you are all that exists. When we begin to transcend the mind we will no longer believe the same thoughts at all. As we begin to transcend all thoughts then our mirror image must also change to reflect the new perspective of ourselves.

Once we see through this myth, we can stop trying to fix our lives before trying to wake up, and we can also stop waiting for enlightenment to fix everything for us or make our life better. In truth, healing our mind, body and life is really the same thing as reaching full enlightenment, there is no difference between the two. Once we come to see clearly what we really are we will notice it having a cleansing effect on all that we experience. Enlightened beings have simply allowed this process to come to its conclusion and they live in total peace as a result.

CHAPTER 11

You Already Have What It takes

After reading and digesting these ten myths, we should be able to stop putting these beings on a pedestal so much and begin to see that awakened beings struggled just like we do. They did not have any special advantages and often have gone through some awful events in their lives. They have had to figure their own way through their awakening just like you are doing. It is time to start living to the fullest possibility you can. It is time for you to realise the true nature of your being and to live in the fullness of that truth. Awakening is possible for anyone willing to consistently do what is needed to reach enlightenment, and now you can begin to see that others that went before you had no special character traits that you don't. They were, and are, just normal human beings that inquired deeply into the nature of reality and themselves. They have not done anything that you cannot do.

There are many more myths that could be included in this book but the essence of each myth remains the same. We have judged what it is like to be enlightened and what it takes to get there by the behaviour of a few beings, and this has led to collectively agreed upon myths in human consciousness. These myths have caused us to feel that we don't have what it takes and that those who have reached enlightenment are somehow different to us or more gifted. It's time to put an end to these myths and write a whole new chapter in humanity where every day, ordinary people wake up to their true nature and live a normal, happy life in peace.

Why not you? Why not now?

APPENDIX

Summary of Common Names for the Noumenon

Below are some of the ways the Noumenon has been described in other teachings. For each set of terms there are two names. Reading through the list may help to awaken a recognition in you as you read and at certain times along the way different sets of terms may be more appealing than others. They are all names for That Which Has No Name. Don't get attached to any name; look at what the name points to.

NOUMENON	PHENOMENA
Oneness	many
Allness	separation
Empty Mind	full mind
Unity	multiplicity
Silent Mind	noisy mind
Non-Duality	duality
"I" as Consciousness	"I" as a person
Nothingness	somethingness
Awakeness	sleep/dream

Consciousness	unconsciousness
Silence	sound
Subjectivity	object
Being	being someone/something
Stillness	movement
Presence	person
God	ego
Truth	falsehood
Formless	form
Reality	illusion
Knowingness	knowing about
Awareness	perception
Context	content
Infinite Field	finite being
Timeless	duration

If you would like more information about Helen, her live Satsangs, silent retreats and classes please contact us:

Website: www.helenhamilton.org

Find us on Facebook by searching:
@satsangwithhelenhamilton

Email us at evolutionofspirit@gmail.com

Search for us on YouTube at "Satsang With Helen Hamilton"

Printed and bound by CPI Group (UK) Ltd, Croydon, CR0 4YY